EDICTS OF THE SYNOD OF PARIS

Chlothar II

King of Franks

Translated by: D.P. Curtin

Dalcassian
Publishing
Company

PHILADELPHIA, PA

ISBN: **978-1-960069-74-0** (Paperback)

Library of Congress Control Number:
Author: Curtin, D.P. (1985-)

Front cover image: Portrait of King Dagobert II of France, 1738, Johann Georg Wille
Book design by J.J. Ripplestick

Printed by Ingram Content Group, 1 Ingram Blvd, La Vergne, Tennessee

First printing edition 2019.

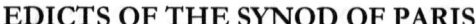

Introduction

The Synod of Paris is a sentinel event in the history of the late Merovingian dynasty. The king was recently capable of reuniting the various Frankish realms under his suzerainty and sought to strengthen royal authority. In the remaining years of his reign, he would go on to call two further councils within his realm for the act of improving the governance of both church and state. However, the Synod of Paris would remain the crowning achievement of his administration and be deeply tied to his legacy for the next three centuries.

Common to the period, but entirely alien to use today, the council was called by the king, who summoned his churchmen to the church of Saint-Pierre de Montmartre in Paris. Future French synods would recall this event in subsequent gatherings, and recount that these edicts held, not only the canonical weight of the church, but the royal authority of the King of France. Second only to perhaps the baptism of Clovis, the Synod of Paris helped forge the union between the French Catholic church and the Crown for the next millennium. All future kings of France would have their royal jurisdiction include that of the church, which would last even beyond the extinction of the monarchy, with the disaster of the disestablishment of the church in France in 1905.

The edicts laid down here are common points of law for the 7th century and extended not only to the questions of the electoral process of a bishop, but also to the courts and points of common law. This synod's status as concilium mixtum grants it special status under French law, as its specific royal edicts technically remain active within the body of French law to this day.

D.P. Curtin
July 21, 2019
Glen Mills, PA

Edicts of the Synod of Paris

There is no doubt that the happiness of our kingdom will increase continually in this, by the divine intercession of the suffrage, if the things in our kingdom, by God's propitiation, which have been well-acted, established, and decreed. Therefore, we endeavor to keep this inviolably in our own time. And those things which have been acted or ordered contrary to the order of reason, so that things which the divinity forbids may not happen beforehand, we have disposed Christ the presbyter, to amend in general, by the tenor of our edict. It is, therefore, our definition of those statutes of the canons that should be preserved in all things, and that which has been omitted through the ages because of this, or from then on, should be perpetually observed.

I. So that, when a bishop dies, in his place, the new candidate must be ordained by the archbishop together with the provincials, as well as be elected by the clergy and the people. If that man is worthy, he shall be consecrated by the ordination of the prince. Or, if not this, he is chosen from the palace, he will be ordered by the merit of his person and his teachings.

II. That none of the bishops, while living, should choose a successor, but then another should be substituted for him, when he was so affected that he could neither govern his church nor the clergy. Also, that no one, living as a bishop, should presume to adopt his place. Yet, if he asks, it shall not be given to him at all.

III. If any cleric, protected by any honor, contemptuous of his bishop, or neglected thereto, shall go to the prince or to a more powerful person whom he has chosen, or to ask for patronage, he shall not be received, unless it appears that he is asking for forgiveness. And if, for any reason, he has sought the prince, and with the prince's letter he has returned to his bishop, he must be excused and received. He who, after the admonition of his priestly office, presumes to retain himself, shall be deprived of holy communion.

IV. So that no judge of any order presumes by himself to arrest or condemn clerics in civil cases, except in criminal matters, unless he is clearly convinced, except another priest or a deacon. Those who have been convicted of a capital crime must be separated according to the canons and examined with the priests.

V. If a case should stand between a public person and the people of the church, the superiors of the churches and the public judge should judge it equally on both sides and place it in a public audience.

VI. To any deceased person, if he has died intestate, the next of kin shall succeed the judge in his capacity according to the law, without opposition to the judge.

VII. Freedmen of any ingenuity from the priests, according to the text of the papers, to defend their ingenuity, and not to be judged, or recalled to the public, without the presence of a bishop or superior of the Church.

VIII. So that wherever a new census is impiously added, and protested by the people, it will be mercifully corrected by a just inquiry.

IX. Of the tribute that should be exacted through those places, or of the very species of which in the time of the preceding princes, that is, until the passage of the good memory of the lords of our fathers, the kings Gunthramni, Chilperic, and Sigebert, it is exacted.

X. The Jews should not take public action over the Christians. Therefore he who presumes to associate himself with a profitable order incurs the most severe law from the canonical sentence.

XI. In order that there may be peace and discipline in our kingdom, through the propitiation of Christ, the perpetual rebellion or insolence of bad men may be severely repressed.

XII. That no judge from other provinces or regions be assigned to other places. So that if he has done something wrong with regard to any condition, he must restore the order of the law according to the order of his own property.

XIII Let our precepts be fulfilled in all things (the end of the chapter is lost.)

XIV. (Text lost.)

XV. (Text lost.)

XVI. Whatever our fathers, the former rulers, or we, have been seen by justice to have conceded and confirmed, ought to be confirmed in all things.

XVII. And which one of the faithful and loyal, in keeping his faith with his lawful master, during the interregnum, was seen to have lost it, we order in general, without any inconvenience, that he is to be restored to the things which were justly due to him.

XVIII. Of religious girls and widows, or holy nuns, who have vowed themselves to God, both those who live in their own houses and those who are placed in monasteries, no one is entitled, neither by our precept, nor to attract, nor to presume to associate with them in marriage. If anyone then utters a precept, there shall be no effect. And if anyone, either by prowess or by any other order, takes them away, or presumes to join them in marriage, let the sentence of capital punishment be struck. If they marry in the church, and she is abducted outright, or abducted so that she appears to consent to this, they shall be exiled from one another, and their possessions shall be shared with their near heirs.

XIX. The bishops, or the powerful magnates, who possess in other regions, do not appoint judges or send disputants from other provinces, except from a place that perceives justice and renders it to others.

XX. Therefore, the agents of the bishops or potentates should not take away the consolations collected by the power of anything, nor should they presume to do the contempt of any of them by themselves.

XXI The tax collectors do not presume to enter the forests of churches or private individuals without the consent of the owner.

XXII. Neither a child nor a servant who is not caught stealing should not be put to death unheard by the judges or by anyone else.

XXIII. When indeed there is no pastureland, so that the pigs cannot be fattened, the cellarers should not be required in public.

XXIV. Whoever, however, presumes to be reckless with this deliberation, which we instituted with the priests, or with such great noblemen, or our faithful in the synodal council. He shall be judged by the sentence of capital punishment himself, as others ought not to perpetrate as he did. Which authority or edict we have resolved to strengthen by the signatures of our hands, which shall prevail for ever and ever.

Given under the 15th day of the month of November, in the 31st year of our reign, Paris.

Hamingus, [Duke of Franks]

Chlotacharius, king in the name of Christ, I subscribed to this definition.

Latin Text

Edictum de synodo Parisiensi

Felicitatem regni nostri in hoc magis magisque, divino intercedente suffragio, succrescere non dubium est, si quae in regno nostro, Deo propitio, bene acta, statuta, atque decreta sunt, inviolabiliter nostro studuerimus tempore custodire; et quae contra rationis ordinem acta vel ordinata sunt, ne inantea, quod avertat divinitas, contingant, disposuerimus, Christo praesule, per hujus edicti nostri tenorem, generaliter emendare. Ideoque definitionis nostrae est ut canonum statuta in omnibus conserventur, et quod per tempora ex hoc praetermissum est, vel dehinc, perpetualiter observetur.

I. Ita ut, episcopo decedente, in loco ipsius, qui a metropolitano ordinari debet cum provincialibus, a clero et populo eligatur; et si persona condigna fuerit, per ordinationem principis ordinetur; vel certe si de palatio eligitur, per meritum personae et doctrinae ordinetur.

II. Ut nullus episcoporum, se vivente, eligat successorem; sed tunc alius ei substituatur, cum taliter afficeretur ut Ecclesiam suam nec clerum regere possit. Itemque ut nullus, vivente episcopo, adoptare locum ejus praesumat. Quod si petierit, ei minime tribuatur.

III. Si quis clericus, quolibet honore munitus, contempto episcopo suo, vel praetermisso, ad principem aut ad potentiores quasque personas ambulare vel sibi patrocinium elegerit expetendum, non recipiatur, praeter si pro venia videtur expetere. Et si pro qualibet causa principem expetierit, et cum ipsius principis epistola ad episcopum suum fuerit reversus, excusatus recipiatur. Is qui ipsum, post admonitionem pontificis sui, retinere praesumpserit, sancta communione privetur.

IV. Ut nullus judicum de quolibet ordine clericos de civilibus causis, praeter criminalia negotia, per se distringere aut damnare praesumat, nisi convincitur manifestus, excepto presbytero aut diacono. Qui vero convicti fuerint de crimine capitali, juxta canones distringantur, et cum pontificibus examinentur.

V. Quod si causa inter personam publicam et homines ecclesiae steterit, pariter ab utraque parte praepositi ecclesiarum et judex publicus in audientia publica positi ea debeant judicare.

VI. Cuicunque defuncto, si intestatus decesserit, propinqui absque contrarietate judicum in ejus facultate juxta legem succedant.

VII. Libertos cujuscunque ingenuorum a sacerdotibus, juxta textus chartarum, ingenuitatis suae defensandos, nec absque praesentia episcopi aut praepositi Ecclesiae esse judicandos, vel ad publicum revocandos .

VIII. Ut ubicunque census novus impie additus est, et a populo reclamatur, justa inquisitione misericorditer emendetur.

IX. De teloneo, ut per ea loca debeat exigi, vel de speciebus ipsis de quibus praecedentium principum tempore, id est, usque ad transitum bonae memoriae domnorum parentum nostrorum Gunthramni, Chilperici, Sigeberti regum, est exactum.

X. Judaei super Christianos actiones publicas agere non debeant. Quare qui se quaestuoso ordini sociare praesumpserit, severissimam legem ex canonica incurrat sententia.

XI. Ut pax et disciplina in regno nostro sit, Christo propitiante, perpetua, rebellio vel insolentia malorum hominum severissime reprimatur.

XII. Ut nullus judex de aliis provinciis aut regionibus in alia loca ordinetur; ut si aliquid mali de quibuslibet conditionibus perpetraverit, de suis propriis rebus exinde quod male abstulerit, juxta legis ordinem debeat restituere.

XIII. Praeceptiones nostrae per omnia impleantur (finis capitis deperdita.)

XIV. (Textus deperditus.)

XV. (Textus deperditus.)

XVI. Quidquid parentes nostri anteriores principes, vel nos, per justitiam visi sumus concessisse et confirmasse, in omnibus debeat confirmari.

XVII. Et quae unus de fidelibus ac leodibus, suam fidem servando domino legitimo, interregno faciente, visus est perdidisse, generaliter absque aliquo incommodo de rebus sibi juste debitis praecepimus revestiri.

XVIII. Puellas et viduas religiosas, aut sanctimoniales, quae se Deo voverunt, tam quae in propriis domibus resident, quam quae in monasteriis positae sunt, nullus nec per praeceptum nostrum competat, nec trahere, nec sibi in conjugio sociare penitus praesumat. Et si quis exinde praeceptum elicuerit, nullum sortiatur effectum. Et si quicunque aut per virtutem aut per quemlibet ordinem ipsas detrahere aut sibi in conjugium praesumpserit sociare, capitali sententia feriatur. Et si in ecclesia conjugium fecerint, et illa rapta aut rapienda in hoc consentire videbitur, sequestrati ab invicem in exsilio deportentur, et facultates eorum propinquis haeredibus socientur.

XIX. Episcopi vero vel potentes, qui in aliis possident regionibus, judices vel missos discussores de aliis provinciis non instituant, nisi de loco, qui justitiam percipiant et aliis reddant.

XX. Agentes igitur episcoporum aut potentum per potestatem nullius rei collecta solatia nec auferant, nec cujuscunque contemptum per se facere non praesumant.

XXI. Porcarii fiscales in silvas ecclesiarum aut privatorum absque voluntate possessoris in silvas eorum ingredi non praesumant.

XXII. Neque ingenuus, neque servus qui cum furto non deprehenditur, a judicibus, aut ad quemcunque interfici non debeat inauditus.

XXIII. Et quando quidem pastio non fuerit, unde porci non debeant saginari, cellarinsis in publico non exigatur.

XXIV. Quicunque vero hanc deliberationem, quam cum pontificibus, vel tam magnis viris optimatibus aut fidelibus nostris in synodali concilio instituimus, temerare praesumpserit, in ipsum capitali sententia judicetur, qualiter alii non debeant similia perpetrare. Quam auctoritatem vel edictum perpetuis temporibus valiturum manus nostrae subscriptionibus decrevimus roborandum.

--Hamingus.
--Chlotacharius, in Christi nomine rex, hanc definitionem subscripsi.

Data sub die XV Kalendas Novembris, anno 31 regni nostri Parisius.

The Scriptorium Project is the work of a small group of lay people of various apostolic churches who are interested in the preservation, transmission, and translation of the works of the early and medieval church. Our efforts are to make the works of the church fathers accessible to anyone who might have an interest in Christian antiquities and the theological, philosophical, and moral writings that have become the bedrock of Western Civilization.

To-date, our releases have pulled from the Greek, Syriac, Georgian, Latin, Celtic, Ethiopian, and Coptic traditions of Christianity, and have been pulled from sundry local traditions and languages.

Other Titles and Translations by D.P. Curtin:

First Book of Ethiopian Maccabees (2018)
Protoevangelium of James: Greek and English Texts (2019)
Edicts of the Synod of Paris by Chlothar II, King of Franks (2019)
The Life of St. Desiderius by Sisebut, King of Visigoths (2019)
The Synod of Rome by St. Boniface IV of Rome (2019)
Letter to Pope Theodore by Victor of Carthage (2020)
The Decree of 610 by Gundemar, King of Visigoths (2020)
Laws of the Church by Dagobert I, King of Franks (2020)
The Old Nubian Miracle of St. Mena (2021)
About Fifteen Problems by St. Albertus Magnus (2022)
Testament of Some Former Things by John Scotus Eriugena (2022)
The Georgian Synaxarium (2022)
Instructions: Counsel for Novices by St. Ammonas the Hermit (2022)
The Syriac Menologium and Martyrology (2022)
Book on Religious Exercise and Quiet by St. Isaiah the Solitary (2022)
Vision of Theophilus by St. Cyril of Alexandria (2022)
On Fate (De Fato) by St. Albertus Magnus (2023)
Fragments of 'Chronicle' by Hippolytus of Thebes (2023)
Life of the Blessed Theotokos by Epiphanius Monachus (2023)
Syriac Life of John the Baptist by Serapion the Presbyter (2023)
Second Book of Ethiopian Maccabees (2023)